O9-BTM-437

DON'T GIVE UP!

DON'T GIVE UP!

JESUS will give You that

Miracle

You need!

By

ORAL

ROBERTS

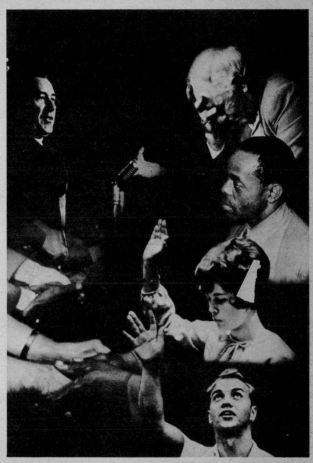

I WROTE THIS BOOK IN THE ARENA OF HUMAN NEEDS AND
HOPELESSNESS . . . NO MATTER HOW BIG YOUR PROBLEMS ARE . . .
DON'T GIVE UP!

TABLE OF CONTENTS

PREFACE

This book is written and dedicated to every person who has ever felt like giving up; it is for everyone facing problems which seem to defy solution. It is a channel, an instrument of faith especially designed and anointed for that person who is being confronted with a broken marriage, problem children, alcoholism, drug addiction, financial disaster, chronic sickness, mental and physical fatigue, spiritual loss or backset, grief, oppression, and depression.

DON'T GIVE UP! This message resounds from every page of God's eternal Word. From Moses to Malachi, from Matthew to John the Revelator, the message springs forth loud and clear: Uncompromising faith is always rewarded! This uncompromising faith is described vividly by the apostle Paul in Hebrews 11:33-37:

33: . . . Who through faith subdued kingdoms, wrought righteousness, obtained promises, stopped the mouths of lions,

34: Quenched the violence of fire, escaped the edge of the sword, out of weakness were made strong, waxed valiant in fight, turned to flight the armies of aliens.

35: Women received their dead raised to life again: and others were tortured, *not accepting deliverance; that they might obtain a better resurrection:*

36: And others had trial of cruel mockings and scourgings, yea, moreover of bonds and imprisonment:

37: They were stoned, they were sawn asunder, were tempted, were slain with the sword . . .

The key line in these four dynamic verses on faith is underlined in verse 35. In other words, they could have spared themselves the ordeal they faced immediately by compromising, but they would have sacrificed the more glorious New Life of the future.

Jesus, who himself was the author and finisher of uncompromising faith, did not give up on humanity, but "for the joy that was set before Him, endured the cross!" He endured the suffering of the crucifixion because He saw the joy of the resurrection.

There is no victory in compromising! Compromising means settling for less, and, in the end, even that is lost because what is gained by compromising is only temporary.

On the other hand, *there is no defeat in faith!* A direct onslaught by hell and all its combined forces cannot vanquish the power of your uncompromising faith.

No one who has ever placed a problem in the hands of God and trusted in Him as the Source of their total supply has received less than heaven's best. No problem is unsolvable and no fear is unconquerable.

I know your needs are pressing and the challenges to your faith are real. But I also know your power potential in God will never reach the peak you desire by giving up!

Ask yourself as you read this book, "Are my problems any greater than these? Are they any more real than these? Can I win by compromising? Can I lose by believing?"

The content of these pages is not theory. It is fact! Absorb every word! When you have finished you will understand why I can say to you now, by the authority of Jesus Christ: YOUR ANSWER IS ON THE WAY . . . DON'T GIVE UP!

Part I

THE FOURTH MAN

three companions, Shadrach, Meshach, and Abednego, were captured and brought to Babylon, he was the undisputed ruler of the world. Here is the story of how these men of God were brought to Babylon:

One day Nebuchadnezzar led his crack legions across the burning sands of the desert and laid siege to Jerusalem, capital of the little kingdom of Judah. It was during a time when the people of God had turned away from the paths of righteousness and had broken their covenant with God. When these people kept their covenant with God no foe could defeat them, no matter how mighty. When they broke their covenant with God they were easy prey for even the weakest enemy. There were a few in the nation who held on to the covenant, but the masses had strayed far from the ways of God. The few suffered with the masses.

With their battering rams the Babylonians tore down the walls of the "City of the Great King," plundered and sacked Jerusalem, destroyed the temple of God, and led captive the very flower of the nation as trophies of their victory. Among these captives were Daniel and the three Hebrew children, Shadrach, Meshach, and Abednego.

While standing on one of the hills overlooking their ravished city, these young Hebrew princes chanted their melancholy psalm: "If I forget thee, O Jerusalem, let my right hand forget its cunning . . . let my tongue cleave to the roof of my mouth."

Weeks later, at the end of their long and torturous trek across the desert, they passed inside the massive walls of Babylon, captives of a heathen king. Curious Babylonians came to gaze upon them as they were led down to the banks of the Euphrates. "Sing us one of the songs of Zion," mocked the Babylonians.

"How shall we sing the song of the Lord in a strange land?" they replied.

It was a strange land indeed. Nebuchadnezzar had gone across the civilized world with his armies capturing the nations and their gods, gods made with human hands, and had brought them back to Babylon where he stockpiled them. As he gazed across this stockpile of man-made gods, he proclaimed that there was no god on earth who could stand before him. Even stranger than these other man-made gods, which Nebuchadnezzar had brought into Babylon, was the one standing on the plain of Dura. It was Nebuchadnezzar's own image cast in gold. The image was enormous. It stood almost 100 feet high and some 10 feet wide. The image of the despotic king was erected solely to satisfy his arrogant pride. It was there to feed his sinful ego by reminding him that he had conquered every nation known to the world at that time. At his every whim he would issue an order demanding all the people in the city to pour into the streets, and, at the sound of music, to fall upon their knees and chant, "Great is Nebuchadnezzar our god, great is Nebuchadnezzar our god."

But deep in his heart Nebuchadnezzar knew there was one nation he had never conquered. Even though he had destroyed its walls, burned its cities, and torn down that nation's temple block by block, its people would still not bow to him. The people of Israel, even in a back-slidden condition, refused to acknowledge him as their god.

Shadrach, Meshach, and Abednego had not back-slidden. They were still in covenant with the God of their father, Abraham. Their law stated plainly, "Thou shalt not bow down to any graven image or worship any idol." While others around them fell on their knees and compromised their faith, these three young men emphatically stood their ground. They would not give up their faith in God.

It didn't take long for that news to reach the palace of the king. He stormed, ranted, and raved. The walls of the mighty palace reverberated with his violence as he racked his brain for a device to make these proud rebels bow their knees to him.

YOUR FAITH WILL BE TRIED

Finally the king, drunk on rage, settled upon a plan. It was carefully, diabolically inspired by the hosts of hell.

There would be a special dedication for the image of Nebuchadnezzar. By royal decree, all the people in the province of Babylon would be required to present themselves and worship his image. For those who chose not to go along with the program, he had something special prepared.

As the Babylonians assembled in the streets, a herald was already crying out the proclamation, "To you it is commanded, O people, nations, and languages, that at the time you hear the music of the cornet, harp, flute, and psaltery, you are to fall down and worship the golden image which Nebuchadnezzar the king has set up."

Now for the something special, "And whoever doesn't fall down and worship the image shall be thrown into the middle of a burning, fiery furnace."

Standing in the middle of that great throng, Shadrach, Meshach, and Abednego came to grips with reality. At that precise moment, they came face-to-face with an inescapable fact of life: TRUE FAITH IN GOD WILL BE TRIED! Whether God's people live in Babylon or the United States or Canada or someplace else, whether they are preachers or lay members, whether they are men or women, they will be tried. Each one will have the opportunity to prove what kind of material his faith is built with.

Young people especially have their faith tested. In one of our crusades a beautiful young lady responded to my altar call. She accepted Jesus Christ as her personal Savior and was gloriously saved. She returned to her seat with shining eyes and a burning heart. She said to her young boyfriend, "What Jesus has done for me this evening is wonderful. Come and go with me to the front. I want you to experience what the Lord has done for me."

He laughed in her face.

For a moment she didn't know what to do or say. But when her young friend continued to make fun and mock the experience she had just had with God, she turned to him, looked him straight in the eye, and said calmly, "All right, if you will not go to heaven with me, I most certainly will not go to hell with you!"

This young lady's faith was made of the right kind of stuff. She knew what she wanted and where she was going. She wanted others to go with her, but one thing was sure: She Would Not Compromise! She was going to heaven, even if she had to go without her young friend. She would not give up her experience with God!

A lady wrote me a letter about her husband who was up and down and in and out in his experience with God. He had made a new commitment to God in one of our crusades and for a few months was on fire for God. "But," the lady wrote, "he is beginning to slip back into his old life-style. I just know if you will let him join your staff, so he can be around you all the time, that he will stay on fire."

What this lady did not realize is: Faith In God Is Not A Thing Of Environment; It is An Attitude Of The Heart. It is an inner peace and power that comes into the core of a person's being by the Holy Spirit.

And it only happens when a person repents of his sins and maintains a right relationship with God. If the Spirit of God indwelling a person's heart is cultivated, He will give him great spiritual strength and cause faith to be ever on the increase.

Religion gives power to a man's life only when he wants to serve God as a matter of principle, when he makes it a life-style. Help may be received from another Christian, but his own faith in God is sufficient for him to live an abundant life in Christ Jesus, no matter what the circumstances, condition, or environment.

Faith in God is not a *gimmick* to be used only when trouble appears in your life. It must become a daily routine. To have your faith reach the level you need, you must daily look to God as your Source of total supply. This is the beginning of SEED-FAITH.

Special dedication or not, Shadrach, Meshach, and Abednego would not compromise. It was not hard for the king's tattlers to spot the Hebrew children; they were the only ones standing on their feet. Everybody else had fallen to his knees in appeasement to Nebuchadnezzar.

Sitting in his palace, the arrogant ruler waited for the word to arrive letting him know whether or not the three Hebrews had been conquered. Swiftly the messenger came into the room. The message was infuriating, "O King, those three young men refused to bow down to your image."

"Bring them to me!" he roared in his fury.

Shortly Shadrach, Meshach, and Abednego appeared and stood before the king. "Is it true that when you heard the sound of the music, you refused to bow to my image?" he asked.

They admitted it was true.

"I'll give you one more chance," Nebuchadnezzar said, "and if, when you hear the music this time, you will fall down and worship my image I will let bygones be bygones; everything will be well and good."

The devil will always go out of his way to give you another chance to give up by compromising your faith. He will try this tactic on you as surely as he did these young men.

The king saw them set their faces like rocks. He knew what their answer was before they opened their mouths.

In today's language I can hear Shadrach say, "Thanks, but no thanks!"

The king could not believe what his ears were hearing. "Do you understand that I have prepared a burning, fiery furnace which has been heated seven times hotter than ever before?" he asked.

They assured him they understood!

"You will either bow to my image or burn in my furnace!" the king roared. What a choice, either bow or burn. *Put yourself in the place of the Hebrew children and your trials and problems in the place of the furnace.* Now look at what is happening in your own life. Is this not exactly what the devil is saying to you through every need you face, "Either you bow and give up by compromising your faith, or I will destroy you with the problems you have."

Nebuchadnezzar continued with his taunts and jeers. "When I captured Jerusalem I could not find your God. I have gods from every nation in the world in my courtyard. Your God has no physical likeness or earthly form. Therefore you have no God. Now I am telling you for the last time. You either bow down to my image, or I will throw you into this furnace. Is your God able to deliver you from the violence of its flame? Who is the God that shall deliver you out of my hands?"

Without a moment's hesitation, without so much as the flicker of an eyelash, they said, "King, we do not care one little bit to give you the answer to that question. We are not intimidated by your threats and we are not afraid of your boasts!"

Can't you just see the thought in Meshach's mind, "You may not be able to see our God, but we sure can feel Him.

"Our God, whom we serve continually, is able to deliver us from both your hand and the burning, fiery furnace. Whether or not it is His plan to do so, we don't know. But we want you to know something either way, we may burn in your furnace, but we will not bow down to your image."

Partner, I want you to know this: You cannot win

by compromising. What is gained by compromising is always lost in the fiery trials of the furnace of life. If you bow to the devil you will burn up in your problems. If you will stand up on your feet and refuse to give up, you cannot lose. God will not let your problems destroy you if you will trust Him completely as your Source of deliverance. You have nothing whatsoever to lose by trusting God because if you don't trust Him you will lose all anyway.

He is able!

Thank God, our God is able!

Let the angels shout it, "Our God is able!"

Let weakness lie limp on His shoulder, "Our God is able!"

Let the heathen rage and the people imagine a vain thing, "Our God is able!"

Let the hosts of hell assail, "Our God is able!"

Let the devil roar in his fury, "Our God is able!"

Let the kings of the earth tremble, "Our God is able!"

Let Nebuchadnezzar heat his furnace seven times hotter than it has ever been, "Our God is able!"

Bring forth the royal diadem, "Our God is able!"

Shadrach, Meshach, and Abednego knew God was able. They were not just saying that to bolster their own courage; they were speaking out of knowledge and experience. The record of their God declared that He was able. The prophets bore witness that He was able. The Psalmist sang it and the children of

Israel danced on the dry sands of the parted Red Sea and shouted that He was able. They remembered His outstretched hand, and His Spirit told them that He was able. They believed this so strongly that their God, invisible though He was, was more real to them than the visible Nebuchadnezzar standing before them boasting his blasphemous claims.

"Our God whom we serve is able!" they shouted. "Our God is able to deliver us out of your hand, O King!"

Nebuchadnezzar had succeeded in locking them inside the mighty walls of Babylon, but even his mighty fortress could not keep their God out. He had isolated them from their native surroundings, but he could not separate them from their God. He had dragged them away from the city of the Great King, but he could not keep the King of kings from going with them.

This was the first time anyone had ever had the courage to tell old blasphemous Nebuchadnezzar the truth about God. He was enraged. He recognized the seed of rebellion and knew that if it were not quenched, his kingdom could not last. Screaming for his most powerful soldiers, he gave the order, "Heat the furnace seven times hotter than it has ever been." He had genuine respect for these servants of God. The soldiers bound Shadrach, Meshach, and Abednego with their clothes on. The king's command was urgent!

THE TERRIBLE PRICE OF COMPROMISE

Now, my friend, we are talking a life or death situation here. The stark reality of what was happening dawned upon these men of God. Negotiating had reached an end . . . it was either put up or shut up for the three Hebrew children.

I can imagine the thoughts racing through their minds as they were bound, hand and foot, and led toward that raging inferno. "This guy is really serious! He is going to throw us into that furnace and those flames are real. This man means business!"

As the furnace door opened up what resembled the very bowels of hell, the violent flame leaped out and began to burn up the soldiers who had moved too close to the fire. The smell of seared flesh filled the air.

Who were these soldiers? They were closest to the king. They represented his most powerful men. They polished his boots and bowed before him and answered to his every beck and call. What did they get out of it? When they got close enough to the flame to feel the intense heat, they were combustible and fragile. They could not endure. Compromisers can never endure. These men lost their human attributes. They had lost self-respect, courage, integrity, and the will to fight back. Those precious qualities had been destroyed in their compromise. Giving up and bowing down took their very dignity. Giving up and bowing down will take your dignity, too!

"Run, or you will die in that furnace," doubt said to the three Hebrews as the soldiers fell dead on the floor.

"Face the flames head-on and you will never regret it," faith said.

Faith won the argument and the young men stood in place as more soldiers ran up to them and cast them, bound, into the burning, fiery furnace. But the flames, which had killed the most powerful men in Nebuchadnezzar's army, had no effect on Shadrach, Meshach, and Abednego.

Instead of being destroyed by the fire, their faith was rewarded by meeting the Son of God face-to-face centuries before He appeared to the rest of the world. He appeared to them as the FOURTH MAN in the midst of the violence of the fire.

As Nebuchadnezzar watched from a safe vantage point, his countenance changed; fear gripped his heart; his mouth got dry and his lips white as he looked into the raging flames. He expected to see the three Hebrews writhing in pain on the floor of the furnace. Instead, his vision fell upon one – two – three – four men walking around in the flames. That couldn't be right! Could it?

"How many men did we throw into the furnace?" he asked, trying to keep his chattering teeth silent.

"Three!" came back the reply.

"Well," the king gasped, "I see *four* men loose and

walking around in there!"

"Who is the fourth man?" somebody asked, running up to take a look.

"I don't know," the king replied, "but He looks like the Son of God!"

Are your problems real? Do you really have needs? The answer to these questions I am sure is, yes. But are they any more real than the burning, fiery furnace into which these young men were thrown?

I know your needs are pressing and I am aware your problems are great. But I know by personal experience that you will never meet the Fourth Man by compromising what you know is truth. If you compromise your faith in God by giving up now, you will be running from the devil the rest of your life. You will spend the rest of your days being dominated and intimidated by the arch enemy of your soul.

If you can only trust God as your Source. If you will make a commitment to Him, enter into a covenant with Him, your faith will take on a new dimension as you meet the incomparable Fourth Man in the fiery trials of life.

There is not one person who does not know what life's fiery furnaces are. They can come in the shape of trouble in the home, they can come through illness, they can come through financial disaster, they can come through a child or spouse who is hooked on the terrible habit of drug addiction or alcoholism. In whatever form they come against your life, they come with all their power.

Oh! How can I describe life's fiery furnaces? Only we, as individuals standing up for God, know what they are because we feel them more than anyone else.

Life's fiery furnaces are here. They are all around us. When we get out of one, another one will be facing us. The missing link in the relationship of God with so many people is their denial of the existence of fiery furnaces. So many people want to serve God without ever having a trial or tribulation. They don't want to suffer the pangs of emotional hurt, which are so keenly necessary for our maturity in Christ Jesus.

Paul understood that. Can you hear him saying, "Oh, that I may know Christ in the fellowship of His sufferings, the power of His resurrection, being made conformable to His death."

It is in these fiery furnaces of life that the Fourth Man appears to us. That is where the action is.

WHO IS THIS FOURTH MAN?

In Genesis, He is the Seed of the Woman.

In Exodus, He is the Passover Lamb.

In Leviticus, He is our High Priest.

In Numbers, He is the Pillar of Cloud by day and the Pillar of Fire by night.

In Deuteronomy, He is the Prophet like unto Moses.

In Joshua, He is the Captain of our Salvation.

In Judges, He is our Judge and Lawgiver.

In Ruth, He is our Kinsman-Redeemer.

In 1 and 2 Samuel, He is our Trusted Prophet.

In Kings and Chronicles, He is our Reigning King.

In Ezra, He is our Faithful Scribe.

In Nehemiah, He is the Rebuilder of the Broken-Down Walls of human life.

In Esther, He is our Mordecai.

In Job, He is our Ever-Living Redeemer. "For I know my Redeemer liveth."

WHO IS THIS FOURTH MAN?

In Psalms, He is our Shepherd.

In Proverbs and Ecclesiastes, He is our Wisdom.

In the Song of Solomon, He is our Lover and Bridegroom.

In Isaiah, He is the Prince of Peace.

In Jeremiah, He is the Righteous Branch.

In Lamentations, He is our Weeping Prophet.

In Ezekiel, He is the Wonderful Four-Faced Man.

And in Daniel, He is the Fourth Man in "Life's Fiery Furnaces."

WHO IS THIS FOURTH MAN?

In Hosea, He is the Faithful Husband. "Forever married to the backslider."

In Joel, He is the Baptizer with the Holy Ghost and Fire.

In Amos, He is our Burden-Bearer.

In Obadiah, He is the Mighty to Save.

In Jonah, He is our Great Foreign Missionary.

In Micah, He is the Messenger proclaiming the Gospel of Peace.

In Nahum, He is the Avenger of God's Elect.

In Habakkuk, He is God's Evangelist, crying, "Revive thy work in the midst of the years."

In Zephaniah, He is our Savior.

In Haggai, He is the Restorer of God's Lost Heritage.

In Zechariah, He is the Fountain Opened in the House of David for sin and uncleanness.

In Malachi, He is the Sun of Righteousness, rising with healing in His wings.

WHO IS THIS FOURTH MAN?

In Matthew, He is the Messiah.

In Mark, He is the Wonder-Worker.

In Luke, He is the Son of Man.

In John, He is the Son of God.

In Acts, He is the Holy Spirit.

In Romans, He is our Justifier.

In 1 and 2 Corinthians, He is the Gifts of the Spirit.

In Galatians, He is the Redeemer from the Curse of the Law.

In Ephesians, He is the Christ of Unsearchable Riches.

In Philippians, He is the God Who Supplies All Our Needs.

In Colossians, He is the Fullness of the Godhead Bodily.

In 1 and 2 Thessalonians, He is our Soon-Coming King.

In 1 and 2 Timothy, He is our Mediator between God and Man.

In Titus, He is our Faithful Pastor.

In Philemon, He is the Friend That Sticketh Closer than a Brother.

WHO IS THIS FOURTH MAN?

In Hebrews, He is the Blood of the Everlasting Covenant.

In James, He is our Great Physician, for, "The prayer of faith shall save the sick."

In 1 and 2 Peter, He is our Chief Shepherd, who soon shall appear with a crown of unfading glory.

In 1, 2, and 3 John, He is Love.

In Jude, He is the Lord Coming with Ten Thousands of His Saints.

And in Revelation, He is the Lord of lords, and King of kings!

WHO IS THIS FOURTH MAN?

He is Abel's Sacrifice, Noah's Rainbow, Abraham's Ram, Isaac's Wells, Jacob's Sceptre, Moses' Rod, Joshua's Sun and Moon that stood still, Elijah's Mantle, Elisha's Staff, Gideon's Fleece, Samuel's Horn of Oil, David's Slingshot, Isaiah's Fig Poultice, Hezekiah's Sundial, Daniel's Visions, Issachar's Burden, and Malachi's Sun of Righteousness.

WHO IS THIS FOURTH MAN?

He is Peter's Shadow, Stephen's Signs and Wonders, Paul's Handkerchiefs and Aprons, and John's Pearly White City.

WHO IS THIS FOURTH MAN?

He is a Father to the Orphan, Husband to the Widow, the Bright and Morning Star to the traveler in the night. He is the Lily in the Valley, the Rose of Sharon, and the Honey in the Rock.

He is the Brightness of God's Glory, the Express Image of His Person, the King of Glory, the Pearl of Great Price, the Rock in a Weary Land, the Cup that Runneth Over, the Rod and the Staff that comfort. And the government of our lives is upon His shoulders.

WHO IS THIS FOURTH MAN?

He is Jesus of Nazareth, the Son of the Living God! Our Savior! Our Companion! Our Lord and our King!

UNTOUCHED BY THE FIRE

The Fourth Man was not responsible for Nebuchadnezzar's infamous act of throwing Shadrach, Meshach, and Abednego into the burning, fiery furnace, but He became responsible for bringing them out. He did not stoke the furnace, but He did rob the fire of its violence. He did not bind the three Hebrew boys, but He did liberate them from their bonds. He did not send them into the furnace, but He did bring them out.

Another thing I want you to see is that the three Hebrew children were freer in the furnace than they were on the outside where compromise was. Before they were cast into the furnace, they were bound; once they were inside, their bonds were burned off. They were thrown down, bound, into the midst of the fire; but when the Fourth Man joined them, they were loose and walking around in the heat of the furnace.

THE KING IS CONVERTED

Nebuchadnezzar shouted, "Shadrach, Meshach, and Abednego, come forth!"

They came forth, rejoicing and praising God. The king began to examine their clothes and bodies. He smelled their hair, felt their clothes, and put his hand to their faces. The smell of fire was not on their garments, neither was the hair of their heads singed.

Because of their love for God, they would not bow.

Because of their faith, God would not let them burn.

By this time the Fourth Man had vanished. He was on His way to deliver someone else who was even then saying, "I will not bow."

Nebuchadnezzar called for his scribes and commanded them to write:

"Blessed be the God of Shadrach, Meshach, and Abednego, who hath sent His angel, and delivered His servants that trusted in Him, and have changed the king's word, and yielded their bodies, that they might not serve nor worship any god, save their own God.

"Therefore, I make a decree, That every people, nation, and language, which speak any thing amiss against the God of Shadrach, Meshach, and Abednego, shall be cut in pieces, and their houses shall be made a dunghill: because there is no other God that can deliver after this sort" (Daniel 3:28,29).

That heathen king had suddenly become a believer. And new convert though he was, his conclusion was as true and profound as any that ever fell from the lips of patriarch, prophet, or sage. For it is a truth as genuine and as eternal as was ever spoken by mortal man: There is no other God that can deliver after this sort.

HOLDING ON TO FAITH PAYS BIG DIVIDENDS. DON'T GIVE UP!

Part II

HEALING ... MY PERSONAL
ACCOUNT OF NOT GIVING UP

I was born Granville Oral Roberts, in Bebee, Oklahoma (a wide spot in the road), the son of Ellis and Claudius Priscilla Roberts. Mamma and Papa were sharecroppers. Being a sharecropper means you do all the work and the man who owns the land gets most all the money. We were so poor, the poor folks called us poor. We did not live on the back side of the world, but we could see it from our back porch.

Five children were born to my parents. I was the youngest. Being born a stutterer with the name "Oral," which means "of speech," caused some problems for me growing up. When I tried to recite in front of my classmates or even talk to my friends, the words would stick in my mouth. My stammering and stuttering made me the laughingstock of the whole school.

"Talk for us, Oral!" the kids would taunt.

"He can't talk," they laughed, "he can't even say his name."

I reacted angrily to them making fun of me. At first I directed my anger toward myself for stuttering, then at the situation which caused me to do it. My life was a cycle of frustration.

The religious convictions of Mamma and Papa did not make my life any easier at that time. Papa had become a part-time preacher in that rural section of Oklahoma, mostly among other poor people. Papa had come from a long line of Methodists. But soon the Holy Spirit began to awaken people to more of the personal presence and power of Jesus. "Pentecostal" power began to fall and my parents embraced it, including healing by faith.

To make matters worse for me, Mamma and Papa kept telling everybody I was going to be a preacher. That confused me because I knew when I tried to talk, I became like I was tongue-tied.

One afternoon while playing with some boys who began to taunt me about my stammering tongue, my frustration reached the boiling point. In utter despair, I ran home and burst into the kitchen where Mamma was. Tears were streaming down my face as I cried out my hurt to her.

Mamma, sitting in an old cane-bottomed chair we had in the kitchen, pulled me close to her breast and said to me, "Oral, I made a covenant with God for your life. I gave you to Him before you were born. One day you will preach the gospel."

By that time we were both crying. I looked up at

Mamma and asked, "M-m-m-mamma, h-h-how c-c-can I-I p-p-p-preach? I-I-I c-c-can't even t-t-t-talk!"

She framed my face with the hardworking hands of an Oklahoma sharecropper's wife and answered, "Son, you are going to preach because God is going to heal you." She would not give up. To everyone else, the idea of stammering, stuttering Oral Roberts ever becoming a preacher was silly, but not to Mamma Roberts.

As I grew into my teens I began to drift away from God and the Methodist church of which I was a member. I rebelled hard against God and the teachings of the church and my parents. I rebelled against the abject poverty in which we lived. I was tired of living in a two-room shack, never having enough clothes, never having enough to eat, my shoes having holes in them and being looked down on by about everybody in the community. I had begun to dream of becoming a lawyer someday. I had to do something to get away.

In the mornings when I went out to feed the chickens and milk the cows, I looked down the dusty farm road, beyond the rolling Oklahoma hills and wondered just what lay in store for me. Anything, I thought, had to be better than this.

At night the heat of the summer was unbearable. There was no such thing as an air conditioner. We didn't even own a fan. As I lay on my bed trying to sleep, I could feel the sweat running down the side of my face; occasionally I could hear the whine of a mosquito and feel its sharp bite. As I lay there looking out the window at the twinkling stars, I made a decision . . . I was leaving home; I would tell Mamma and Papa in the morning.

I had my speech all planned. I was going to box up my few belongings and bravely walk in and tell them, "I am going out into the world and make it on my own. I am going to walk through that door and down the dusty road of life. I don't know where I am going or exactly what I am going to do, but don't worry, I'll make it. I am a man now. I have been wanting to leave for some time, but last night I made up my mind. Today is the day, my day to start toward the dream of a new life." In my mind I could see Mamma and Papa being hurt, but finally wishing me well and sending me off with best wishes.

It was the enemy of my soul who made me run from Papa's preaching and Mamma's prayers. I understand the battles of the young people of today. I know how they feel "turned-off" by the church, the establishment, their parents, and society. As a teenager I felt all of the same nagging emotional pains they feel.

Many nights, as I lay in bed listening to their prayers for my brothers, Elmer and Vaden, and my sister, Jewel, and me, I felt their love as though it was coming right through the walls. But Satan fought me day and night. My thoughts were filled only with running away.

My going-away speech was not as flowery as I planned and Mamma and Papa did not react the way I had imagined. They were hurt all right. I could see the hurt in Papa's eyes. But he didn't have any well-wishes for me.

"Oral," he said, "if you run away I'll send the police after you. They will find you and bring you back."

Angry, I struck back, "It won't do any good, Papa, I'll just run away again."

Mamma came over to me. I was getting tall, already over six feet. Mamma put her hands on my shoulders, looked full into my face and said, "Oral, you can't outrun my prayers. I know Papa and I don't have anything to offer you except love, a home, and raising you right. I won't try to stand in your way because I know you have made up your mind to leave and I can't stop you. But wherever you go, my prayers will be there for you. I will pray until God sends you back."

I walked across the room, pushed that old screen door open, and let it slam behind me. The old gray, faded planks squeaked as I stepped off the front porch into the yard. I turned around and saw Papa and Mamma looking at me through the screen door with all the love and compassion a parent could feel for a child. Mamma's tears where she had kissed me were still wet on my cheeks.

As I walked down the road toward my long-awaited freedom, the very hills seemed to echo what Mamma told me, "Oral, you'll never outrun my prayers. I will pray until God sends you home." This thing was not proceeding exactly like I thought it was going to. But I was determined and kept walking.

At that time we were living in Ada, Oklahoma, the county seat of Pontotoc County in which I had been born. I went to Atoka, Oklahoma, where I secured a room with a judge's family. After dinner each evening I was allowed to study the judge's law books. I went through these books with all the hunger of a young animal searching for food. I dreamed in my mind, while clutching those law books in my hand, of someday becoming a lawyer and then going on to become the governor of the state of Oklahoma.

To support myself I followed a very demanding schedule. I served as a handyman in the home of the judge. I took a job at a grocery store on Saturdays, threw a paper route, and wrote a column and served as a reporter for my hometown newspaper, *The Ada Evening News*.

I arose each morning at 4:00 a.m. and built the fires. I went to bed around midnight after I finished the day's classes, practiced basketball, threw my paper route, wrote my column, and maybe even had a date. In school I carried a full load too. I loved to study and was an A student.

When I left Mamma and Papa's home and started down that dusty road, I was determined to make something of myself. I was working very hard at doing just that. In spite of my stuttering, I was elected president of my class and made the starting lineup on the basketball team.

But I was pushing myself beyond my physical capabilities. Besides being born a stutterer, I was also born with very weak lungs. I began having small pains in my chest and waking up at night in deep sweats. I started tiring easily, and many times after a basketball game it felt as if my lungs were going to explode. Every now and then I spat up blood when I coughed, but I thought nothing of it. I was excited by what was going on, fascinated by life, and getting more confident every day. I saw nothing but my future before me and nothing could stop me.

My whole world came crashing down around me one night in the final game of the southeastern Oklahoma basketball tournament. The ball was passed to me! I moved around the man guarding me and dribbled down the court! The crowd was on its feet cheering me on! The roar was deafening as I dribbled across the floor and drove in for a lay-up as hard and fast as I could.

Suddenly . . . everything began to blur before my eyes; I stumbled and collapsed on the gymnasium floor; blood began running out of my mouth; I lost consciousness briefly and began hemorrhaging with every breath. My coach, Mr. Herman Hamilton, rushed over to me and soon he and some of the

players and fans carried me out to his car and laid
me on the back seat. "Oral," he said, "I'm taking you
home."

I was so afraid as I lay in Coach Hamilton's car
looking out into the night. All my hopes, my dreams
for the future, my ambitions were dashed to pieces
in minutes. I did not know what was wrong, but I
knew whatever it was, was bad. I also knew I was
heading back to poverty, back to a religious home
I had never accepted, back to my parents' strict disci-
pline, and it crushed me inside.

When we pulled up in Mamma and Papa's front
yard, Coach Hamilton went up to the front door and
knocked. (By this time Papa was pastoring a small
church.)

"Reverend Roberts?" I heard him say.

"Yes," my father answered, "is something wrong?"

Coach Hamilton said, "Reverend Roberts, I've
brought your son home. Can you help me carry
him in?"

When Mamma saw Papa and my coach carrying
me in, she cried, "O God! I didn't know he would
come home like this!"

They carried me into the bedroom and put me
into bed. Although most Pentecostals at that time
believed strongly in divine healing and had very little
to do with doctors or the medical profession, my dad
was an exception. The doctors were called in and
began making their examinations. The pain in my

lungs was terrible. At night I coughed and hemorrhaged so much that eventually the wallpaper beside
my bed had to be removed and new wallpaper put on.

One day after the doctor had examined me and
left, Papa came into my room. Tears welled up in
his eyes as he tried to speak to me.

I said, "Papa, what's wrong?"

He said, "Son, you are going to be all right."

"Well," I said, "if I'm going to be all right, why
are you crying?"

Papa replied, "You're going to be all right, Son."

I knew something dreadful was wrong. I said,
"Papa, tell me the truth. What is wrong with me?
Why do my lungs hurt? Why do I cough up blood?
Why do I not want to eat anymore?"

What he said to me chilled me to the bone. My
world collapsed as he tearfully blurted out, "Oral, you
have tuberculosis in both lungs."

I could not believe it, but he assured me it was
true. I had tuberculosis and was to be sent to the
state tubercular sanitorium at Talihina, in the mountains of eastern Oklahoma.

This was 1935. In those days there was no peni-
cillin, no so-called miracle drugs, and to have tuberculosis at the age of 17 was a much greater threat than
it would be today. Relatives of mine had died with
tuberculosis. My oldest sister, Velma, had died at 19
of pneumonia. The stark reality of death was staring
me in the face.

When my brother Vaden was told, he came in crying and flung himself across the bed, asking God to let him have the disease instead of me. I finally pushed him off me and reached over to the nightstand where my medicine was. I picked up the medicine and said, "Here, Papa, take this away from me."

"What do you mean, Oral?" Papa asked.

I said, "Papa, if there is no cure for tuberculosis, I am going to die, and this medicine isn't going to do any good." I was giving up!

Mamma came into my room, took my hand, and started talking to me. I finally stopped her by saying, "Mamma, what did your daddy die of?"

She looked down at me, but she would not answer.

Again I said, "Mamma, answer me. What did your daddy die of?"

Finally she answered, "He died of tuberculosis!"

Can you imagine how I felt. This only confirmed my fears that I, too, was going to die. I lay there day after day questioning why this should happen to me. What had I done to deserve this?

Mamma, however, was convinced that God was going to heal me and she urged my father to write everyone we knew to pray and believe God for my healing. She just would not give up. Sometimes entire groups of these friends would come to stay with us a day or two to pray for me. It all seemed like a dream. I looked at them through eyes that really didn't see and heard them through ears that really didn't hear.

I talked often with my mother about my future, about being a lawyer. She would smooth my pillow, put her hand on me or lean over and kiss my brow, and say, "We'll see, son, we'll see."

Each time I looked into her face, I remembered the many times she had held me close and told me that someday I would be a preacher. Then I began to grow bitter that my lungs were bursting inside, that I had fever nearly all the time, and that when I tried to stand and walk I was so weak that I stumbled and fell and had to have Mamma and Papa pick me up and put me back on the bed.

Papa finally accepted an appointment at a smaller church in Stratford, Oklahoma, 18 miles to the west of Ada, so he could be with me all the time. People by the dozens came and went. They came to see the preacher's boy who lay dying with tuberculosis at such a tender age. Some came to pray, some just came to show sympathy.

When Papa and Mr. Hamilton, the basketball coach, had put me into bed I weighed 160 pounds and had a 6-foot 1½-inch frame. After lying bedfast for 163 days my weight dropped to 120 pounds. My friends could no longer recognize me. In fact, when they came to visit me, they could hardly stand to look at me; I had bedsores from lying in bed so long.

My food tasted like wood. Sharp pains were constantly in my chest now. The pains ran clear through to my shoulder blades. Night sweats were constant, and the bloody, hacking cough was always there. I began to curse the day I was born. I was giving up.

I had a lot of medicine; some, prescribed by doctors and some, home remedies, prescribed by well-meaning friends.

Constant prayers were said over me, and from time to time predictions were made that the end for me was near. Except for the suffering in my body, I lived in a state of unreality. My mind was in a shadow and it felt as though I was far away from normal things.

I didn't respond to my parents' entreaties to pray or to let Christ become more real to me. A stupor engulfed me, and at last, it was as though I didn't see or hear anyone. I refused to take any more medicine, saying, "If I'm going to die anyway, why take that bitter-tasting stuff?"

My pastor from our Methodist church came to visit and pray with me. I had kept my membership in the Methodist church even though my father had become a Pentecostal Holiness minister. Most of my young friends were Methodist. But now, as my pastor started to leave, he said, "Oral, you've just got to be patient."

I had never been patient, even when well, and now I was certainly not interested in patiently waiting to die. "Brother," I thought, "if this is all the Lord has to offer, I don't want Him."

My parents' religion was equally repelling. Folks would gather in my parents' home and discuss my case. I could hear them talk from where I lay dying. On and on they would go with their opinions about why I was sick. They would come into my room, pray for me and say, "Oral, God loves you. Let Him have your life." But when they went into the other room, their stories seemed to change. They all seemed to agree on one thing: God had stricken me with this killing disease. I was so confused. I could not figure out why God, if He loved me, would do such a thing to me. Why would He want me struck down like this?

These people would talk to me about going to heaven. They found it very difficult to appreciate my response: "I'm not interested in dying and going to heaven, nor am I interested in dying and going to hell. I am interested in living and getting well."

One Sunday evening Papa sent one of his deacons word to take that evening's service. I knew something was going on. I said to Papa, "Are you not going to church tonight?"

"No," Papa replied, "I am not going to church. Oral, I am not giving up on you. I am going to get on my knees and pray until I hear from heaven."

Now that I have children of my own, I can appreciate Papa's grim determination not to let the devil kill his baby boy. Papa knelt at the foot of my bed and leaned across it. He's with Jesus now, after having lived 87 years, but I can still hear him praying for me and see him on his knees at the end of my bed. I don't ever remember Papa praying as hard as he prayed that night. When he raised his head from my bed the front of his shirt was drenched with his tears.

What happened next was the beginning of a series of events that led to my healing and being called into the ministry of healing. Suddenly, while Papa had his hands raised and his face looking upward, my eyes blinked wide open in total amazement, my heart beat faster, my mouth gaped — in place of my father's face was the face of the Lord Jesus Christ. I can't tell you what went racing through my mind, but I can tell you that hope surged in my heart.

The second dramatic event took place in the grocery store while Mamma was shopping. As she walked down the aisle of the market picking up a few things for us to eat, she began to weep. By the time she got to the cash register, tears were dripping off her tired face. As she fumbled, trying to open her little change purse, the groceryman said, "Mrs. Roberts, I can't help but notice your tears. Why are you crying? Did Oral die?"

"No, sir," Mamma said, "these are not tears of sorrow, they are tears of joy. God just gave me the assurance Oral is going to be healed! My son is going to get a miracle from the Lord Jesus!" The groceryman had given up. He expected me to die at any time. He just figured it had finally happened. But

Mamma never did give up! My mother, I don't think I have ever seen a woman with more determination. She had the look of eagles in her eyes. She never did doubt that God would keep the covenant she made with Him before my birth.

The third thing which stirred me inwardly happened through my sister Jewel. Jewel lived in Ada, 18 miles away. One afternoon she had an uncontrollable urge to come to our house. When she got there she walked straight into my room, looked down into my face, and preached the most dynamic faith sermon I have heard to this very day. I say that because she preached it straight to me. It wasn't very long. In fact, it only contained seven words. But to me, those words were the greatest I had ever heard. Now you must remember, sermons had not reached me! Beautiful hymns had not reached me! The church people had not reached me! What Jewel said shook me from center to circumference. She said, "Oral, God is going to heal you!" Through those seven words Jesus was identified to me. He became part of my life, my future, my very existence. He knew I existed. I was a person to Him, a human being worth saving. It was at that moment I realized Jesus was concerned about me!

Even though I was born with a stuttering, stammering tongue, He cared about me! Even though I had run away from home, He cared about me! Even though I had turned my back on Him and my parents and had forsaken their teachings, He cared about me! He had known about me all the time; He was going to heal me! Thank God that Jewel and the rest of my family never gave up on me. THEY HELD ON TO GOD FOR ME, WHEN I COULD NOT HOLD ON FOR MYSELF.

Not long after Jewel had spoken those seven words of deliverance to me, I lay, still very sick, in my bedroom. The sun was just setting on the hills behind our house when I heard the sound of a car. I listened as the car pulled up into our driveway. The brakes gave a loud squeak and the engine stopped. The door slammed shut and footsteps began approaching our porch. I heard the thump . . . thump . . . thump of heavy shoes walking across the porch and the screen door creaking open. Slam! The door shut and the steps neared my room; around the door, into my room stepped my oldest brother Elmer.

Elmer said to me, "Oral, get up and get dressed!"

"Elmer," I said, "I can't get up. I am too weak."

He said, "I'll help you get up."

Mamma and Papa, who were in the other room, heard the voices and came in. "Why, Elmer," Papa said, "what are you doing here?"

"I have come to get Oral. There is a tent meetin' over in Ada, and the preacher is praying for sick people and they're gettin' healed. Ory (Elmer's wife; her name was Ora, but country folks pronounced it "Ory") took me down to the meetin' and I saw people

I know gettin' healed. Oral, I saw it with my own eyes."

I couldn't figure out what had happened to Elmer. I was only about five years old when he had married and moved away, so I didn't know him real well, but I knew he wasn't any more religious than I was. Something had definitely happened to make Elmer get this excited about a revival meeting.

He kept on telling me what he had seen on the previous nights of the revival. "Oral," he said, "this preacher prays for everything. After he prays, people testify that they feel better. He preaches different than what we've heard. He tells all about faith and how God can heal people of all kinds of sickness. Last night while I was sittin' there watchin' all those people get healed, I told Ory I was goin' to bring you and let you get healed too. Now get dressed!"

This announcement Elmer made didn't seem to surprise Mamma too much. "Well," she said, "I knew God was going to heal him." Like I said, Mamma just did not give up.

"Where did you get that car?" Papa asked.

"I borrowed it!" Elmer said, "And I took the last 35 cents I had to buy gas."

Elmer worked at the flour mill. He made about $10 per week. That 35 cents was all he had left until payday. (Gasoline was 14 cents a gallon at that time.)

"Well, let's get him dressed and get him down there," Papa said.

They all helped me get out of bed and started dressing me. I had only one suit. I had bought that one when I weighed 160 pounds. When they put my clothes on me, the suit literally hung on my body. I wrapped it around me. They put my shoes on me and Elmer carried me, mattress and all, and put me in the back seat of that borrowed car. We couldn't afford an ambulance to take me to the meeting.

As Elmer stepped off the porch with me in his arms, I saw determination in his eyes; determination to get his baby brother some help . . . even if it meant spending his last 35 cents for gas! The thought ran through my mind then, "Elmer really loves me." Elmer hadn't given up. It felt so good to have him hold my sick body with the love and compassion he was showing toward me. It felt good just to realize my family had not given up!

Elmer, Mamma, and Papa got into the front seat after putting me in the back seat. Down the road we went, that old car bouncing in the ruts and the dust flying. Just a few months before, I had gone down the same road toward what I thought was my freedom. This time, though I didn't know it then, I was going down the road toward my personal appointment with destiny!

As I rode along, listening to my family's conversation and the rattle of the gravel hitting on the bottom of the car, the sound of the gravel, the conversation, and the roar of the motor began to fade away.

Those sounds were replaced with another kind of sound, gradually increasing in volume, coming from within me! My entire being was filled with that sound! Suddenly, from within, the voice of God began to speak! My whole body seemed to fill up with His voice, speaking not only in me but to me, "Son, I am going to heal you, and you are to take the message of My healing power to your generation."

I didn't understand all God was saying but it helped me endure the long ride to the tent revival in Ada. I was so sore in my body that each bump the car hit sent pain racing through me. When we arrived, the tent was already overflowing. In a special section a multitude of sick people lay on cots, sat in wheelchairs, sat holding crutches and canes. Mothers held their sick babies; some even had nightclothes on.

Papa got out of the car first. He went inside and found an empty rocking chair with pillows on both sides. They carried me in and sat me down. The service began!

Elmer was right! This church service was different than the ones we had been used to. There was something "electric" in the air. In later years, of course, I would come to know this feeling as the divine presence of the Holy Spirit. The preacher's words were charged with this feeling; his eyes flashed with authority as he spoke the miraculous Name of Jesus Christ of Nazareth.

Up to that point, my family had held on for my

healing. Now I was holding on. I did not know one man could preach as long as that preacher did. I could hardly wait for him to get to the part of the service where he prayed for the sick. Finally, he got around to that! He prayed for everybody in the tent! Everybody, that is, but me! It was getting close to midnight. I thought he would never pray for me, but I wasn't doubting God. He had spoken to me on the way to this very service. Whether this preacher prayed or not, I believed I was going to get healed.

Just when I thought he wasn't going to get to me to pray, he walked over to me. He looked me straight in the eye. Then he prayed, "YOU FOUL DISEASE, I COMMAND YOU, IN THE NAME OF JESUS CHRIST, COME OUT OF THIS BOY'S LUNGS. LOOSE HIM AND LET HIM GO!"

I had never heard a prayer like that. I had never felt such authority from a man. The only prayers I had heard for my healing began, "Lord, if it be thy will . . ." This man wasn't playing around. He meant business!

While I listened to him praying I felt something. It started at the bottom of my feet and moved up my legs. Soon it was flooding my chest and my whole body. I felt strength flowing into my weakened diseased body. I had learned to breathe from the top of my lungs because when I took deep breaths I hemorrhaged badly. But now, as the healing Spirit of the Lord surged through my body, I began taking deep breaths! I was breathing to the bottom of my lungs! This was more than I could comprehend. All at once I leaped up and shouted to the top of my voice, "I am healed! God has healed me!" I raced back and forth on the platform and just kept shouting as loudly as I could, "I am healed! I am healed! I am healed!"

When I finally settled down, which took a little while because the Roberts family was having its own personal revival, the preacher came over to me smiling. He took hold of my arm and said, "Son, tell the people what the Lord has just done for you."

All of my life I had been a stutterer. I would freeze on the spot when faced by crowds. In school if I had to give an oral book report in front of the class, I would stutter so badly that I would sometimes have to sit down from embarrassment. But that night, when I took the microphone from his hands, I spoke to that crowd like it was my revival. My tongue was loose! I could talk! I could breathe all the way down without coughing or hemorrhaging. I walked up and down the platform telling the people, over the microphone, exactly what Jesus of Nazareth had done for me.

All the way home that night, my thoughts kept going back to how Mamma held me in her arms as a stuttering child chased home by taunting classmates and told me, "Son, you are going to preach the gospel. Jesus is going to heal you."

Words cannot express how happy I was that

Mamma didn't give up . . . Papa didn't give up . . . Elmer didn't give up . . . Jewel didn't give up . . . Vaden didn't give up . . . and I didn't give up! Months of holding on to Mamma's covenant with God were rewarded that spring night.

I was healed completely of tuberculosis in the meeting. However, it took me several weeks to get my strength back. During that time the enemy confronted me again with giving up. This time, *my* faith was challenged to give up on my healing.

One afternoon I sat outside our little house, leaning up against the wall. I was confused about whether or not I had really gotten healed. I could not understand why, if I was healed, I did not get my strength back. About that time Mamma walked around the corner of the house. She came over to me and said, "Oral, you're wondering if you really did get healed, aren't you?"

"Mamma," I said softly, "I'm awfully weak and tired. What if I didn't get healed?"

"Son," she said, "that is the devil trying to discourage you and make you give up. You remember one thing as long as you live: Think about how you felt when the man of God prayed for you in the Name of Jesus. You received healing then. But you have been sick for months. You have lost your strength while lying in bed. It will take you some time to get it back."

Time proved she was right. It took a little while

but I eventually felt my strength returning, and within two months of my healing I delivered my first sermon. It was more like a testimony but it had God's Word in it too. Two souls were saved from hearing that short message.

Later, my parents took me to the Sugg Clinic in Ada, Oklahoma. There my lungs were fluoroscoped by Dr. Morry, who told me, "Son, your lungs are sound as a dollar. You just forget you ever had tuberculosis." Later samples of my blood and spittle were sent to the Oklahoma State Hospital. The report: No tuberculosis found!

From poverty to a runaway . . . from deathbed to healing . . . it all combined to make me a preacher. My first sermon was small, but it was a start. I often think about what would have happened if, while leaning up against the house, I had accepted the doubt, given up my healing, reclaimed the tuberculosis, and gone back to bed. I believe that I would have never risen from that bed again.

The millions of souls who have been saved, the hundreds of thousands of sick bodies who have been made well, all the many seeds of faith we have been able to plant, the hundreds of thousands of phone calls to the Prayer Tower and the millions of letters to this ministry over the years, Oral Roberts University, the City of Faith . . . what would have happened to all these had I given up and gone back to my deathbed?

This chapter of my life closed and another chapter opened, allowing me, with our team, to evangelize the free world, build the Oral Roberts University, and break the ground upon which the City of Faith, now under full construction, will open in 1981, because I Refused To Give Up!

In our crusades in the big tent and auditoriums, we often sang Stuart Hamblen's great song, "It is no secret what God can do. What He's done for others, He'll do for you . . ." And we still sing it. Have faith in God. The same Jesus who delivered me from the bed of affliction and death will deliver you too.

DON'T GIVE UP ! ! !

The moment you decide to give up, you start losing. Let me impress this thought into your mind: NO MATTER WHAT KIND OF PROBLEM YOU FACE . . . FROM A BROKEN HOME TO A BROKEN HEART . . . FROM BROKEN HEALTH TO A BROKEN FINANCIAL CONDITION . . . TO BROKEN FAITH . . . REMEMBER, THE GOD WHO TOOK A BOY DYING WITHOUT HOPE FROM TUBERCULOSIS AND PERFORMED A MIRACLE IN HIS LIFE THEN . . . WHO IS PERFORMING MIRACLES IN HIS LIFE NOW . . . AND WHO IS GOING TO CONTINUE PERFORMING MIRACLES IN HIS LIFE, WILL PERFORM MIRACLES FOR YOU, TOO! I DO NOT FEEL I WAS ANY-

THING SPECIAL, BUT I LEARNED GOD IS A GOOD GOD.

NOTHING IS TOO BIG FOR GOD AND NOTHING IS TOO GOOD FOR YOU!

DON'T GIVE UP – REACH UP! THE ANSWER IS AT YOUR FINGERTIPS!

Part III

LEARNING TO TRUST GOD
FOR FINANCES

THE NIGHT THE DEVIL PRESSED ME
TO GIVE UP

I remember one time in the very early part of our ministry when I closed my Bible, walked off the platform, and said, "I'm through . . ."

It was November 1947. I was preaching a crusade in a city auditorium in Kansas. People were coming to the crusade from a three-state area. There was a great spirit in the meetings. The people were responding to the invitation to accept Christ as Savior and Lord, and many were receiving healing for their illnesses and problems. There was only one thing wrong — the crusade expenses were not being met. As we neared the close of the crusade the money for the rent of the auditorium was not in hand, and I became very distressed. There had been times before this when Evelyn and I had done without in order to pay the bills in connection with our ministry.

The mistake I made this time was to brood and worry instead of looking to God, the Source of my TOTAL supply. (This of course was before I really

The devil almost caused me to give up before I learned the principles of Seed-Faith and my covenant rights.

The Memorial Auditorium in Chanute, Kansas, where early in this ministry God gave us a miracle through my wife Evelyn that kept me from giving up.

understood my covenant rights and the miracle of Seed-Faith.)

I took it as a personal failure of my ability to trust God. I allowed it to develop into a matter between God and me. The more I thought about the rent coming due and not having enough funds on hand to pay it, the more disturbed I became. I felt if I could not trust God for finances, how could I continue to trust Him for souls to be saved and the sick to be healed? If the Lord had really sent me to the people with the message of His healing and delivering power, I reasoned, and if He expected me to be His instrument, I had every right to expect sufficient funds to be raised to meet the obligations incurred by the ministry. I could not bear to think of closing the crusade and leaving the city with the bills unpaid. I would sell every personal thing I had — my car, my clothes, everything if need be — to pay those bills. Anything less was a contradiction to all I was and stood for in integrity and faith.

In spite of my thoughts, nothing changed. The crowds were large and enthusiastic, the spirit was high, and the results were miraculous. Still, we fell further behind in the crusade budget.

One evening I was waiting behind the curtain to be announced to preach. My brother Vaden was standing near me. All at once something broke within me and I said to him, "I am through."

He said, "What's wrong?"

I said, "I don't have the faith and God is not helping me."

He said, "Well, Oral, this is a wonderful crusade."

I said, "Yes, but we can't pay the bills, and you know that Papa always taught us to be honest and pay our bills."

I said, "Vaden, I have done everything I know to do. I have preached the gospel, prayed for the sick, and people have come to God. Now we can't even pay the rent on this building. I can't continue and be honest.

"I am through.

"It is all over.

"I am giving up.

"I am going home."

Vaden left and quickly returned with Evelyn. She was as white as a sheet. She knew when I said something I meant it. And there behind the curtain she put her arms around me and said, "Oral, I know it's hard but you can't quit now. The services are too good and the people are turning more to the Lord every day."

"Evelyn, you know my vow. You and I both promised God that we would never touch the gold or the glory, but we have to have enough to meet our budget. You know it, and I know it. I have prayed to God but He has not heard me. If I am to continue in this ministry God will meet our needs. If not, I am going home."

She said, "Oral, why don't you go out there and tell the crowd how you feel? Maybe they will do more."

I said, "No. God knows my needs. If I can't trust Him for this, how can I trust Him for the other things?"

She said, "Aren't you going to preach tonight?"

I said, "No, it's all over."

She and Vaden left. Pretty soon I heard her talking to the crowd. For a moment it startled me. She had never done this before. In fact, she always said, "When I stand up in front of an audience my mind sits down." But this time she was really talking.

I looked through the curtains. The people were looking at each other and wondering what the evangelist's wife was doing in the pulpit. Moving over to where I could see as well as hear, I heard her say:

"Friends, you don't know what it means for me to stand up here tonight in my husband's place. And I am sure you don't know him as I do. He has come here by faith. No one is responsible for the financial needs to be met except him and God. He has preached and prayed for you and your loved ones each evening, but tonight he feels like quitting. Some of you have not realized your responsibility in supporting this ministry. We can't even pay the rent on the building. Whatever you may think of Oral, there is this about him that you must know. He is honest and if he cannot pay the rent he will not go on. He will not blame you. He will take it as a sign that God does not want him to continue his ministry, and he will stop. I know God has called him and that he must continue to obey God. I am asking you to help him. Together we can save this ministry."

As she spoke, big tears splashed down her face, and I felt smaller and smaller.

"What kind of a man am I," I asked myself, "who would give up when the going gets tough? This is probably a very little trial compared to what I will face in the future." (Little did I realize at that moment how really BIG problems can get!)

These and other questions raced through my mind. Still, I could not change my mind. It was a point of integrity. God had called me, and my needs had to be met. I had heard of others leaving unpaid bills behind, bringing a reproach on the Lord's work, but I would either pay the bills or I would not preach.

I heard Evelyn say, "Maybe some of you don't know we are in need. Perhaps you are waiting for my husband to say more about it. He won't say any more about it. He won't say any more, for his trust is in God. Now I'm going to do something I've never done in my life. I want some man here to lend me his hat, and I'm going to take a freewill offering for the rent."

Several men volunteered their hats. Evelyn selected a big-brimmed black one. Holding the hat close to her, she bowed her head and prayed. I could tell she was embarrassed. Still, *she would not give up*, she was determined to save my ministry. She said:

"All right, now, the Lord and you must help us. Not just for people here who have need of healing, but for people in other places and lands. I am coming among you to pass the hat. I ask God to help you do your part and to bless you for helping us."

Oh, how small my faith was that night. I did not expect Evelyn to succeed. It seemed I had swung too far from the shore and it was time I was striking for home. The devil whispered, "Well, you have sunk pretty low. When you have to let your wife take the offering, it's time you gave up."

Listening to the devil and knowing Evelyn felt like dropping through the floor, I knew I was near total defeat, I actually was blaming God. The truth was that by not understanding my covenant right and remembering who is the Source for my TOTAL supply I was letting God down, as well as myself.

We needed only $300 but it was as large in my mind as a sum ten times larger. It was at this moment that the hand of the Lord touched me. This is a sensation that is difficult to put into words, but I always know and recognize it when it comes to me. It is this touch that changes me from Oral Roberts the man, to a God-anointed servant.

Suddenly a man stood up in the audience and asked Evelyn for permission to say a word. He was a Jewish businessman who had been attending the

services and we had taken a meal in his home. He
had been deeply impressed with the crusade and we
were praying for him. He said:

"Folks, you all know me. I am not a Christian, but
if I ever am, these people (gesturing toward the platform) have what I want. I have some money I owe
the Lord. I'm starting this offering with $20."

Evelyn just stood there and waited. Suddenly a
large red-haired woman stood and said, "I'm ashamed
of everyone in this audience, especially of myself. I'm
the mother of several children. We have lots of needs
and the Lord has helped us get many of these needs
met through His servant, Oral Roberts. Now you
listen to me; I want every one of you to do what I'm
going to do." Then she opened her purse, pulled out
a worn dollar bill, put it in the hat, and sat down. In
a few moments people were standing and saying,
"Mrs. Roberts, bring that hat over here."

As Evelyn went through the crowd, holding out
the black hat with the big western brim, I was thor-
oughly ashamed of myself. When she had finished
with the offering, I had the courage at last to step to
the platform. I was conscious that every eye was
upon me. I had no idea whether enough had been
raised to meet the rent. A new feeling was taking
possession of me. My wife had done something few
wives would have had courage to do for their hus-
bands. I knew she had not done this only for me. A
team of wild horses could not have pulled her up

there. She had willingly gone before the people because she felt the ministry, which she knew God had given me, was endangered. I was proud of her and ashamed of myself for letting doubt and fear creep into my mind . . . that feeling of giving up.

When the need was fully met, I knew that it was an answer from God to me personally. It was also a gentle rebuke. When I stepped forward to take over the service I made no reference whatever to what Evelyn had done, feeling that I could only atone for it by taking my Bible and again preaching the gospel and praying for the people. I read my text and began to preach. I tell you I felt like the power of Niagara had been released in me. I knew that the tide had changed. This meeting ended with a packed house and with the audience standing en masse, urging us to return for another crusade.

I am sure that when GOD gives out the credit for the success of this crusade, more of it will be due my wife than to me. The thing she did that night meant more to me than raising the funds to pay the bills. It proved to me again that Evelyn was my helpmeet — truly a gift from God — and He had used Evelyn in a miracle that saved this ministry. SHE DIDN'T GIVE UP.

WHEN YOU ARE THREATENED

There just isn't any way to get through life without having your very existence threatened. And it's strange how something like unpaid rent can become such a great threat.

The fact is the devil knows where you are vulnerable, your weakest point. He hits you there and keeps on hitting trying to get you to give up.

Jesus called this "facing a mountain . . ." Mountains come in different sizes and shapes and in Jesus' reference they refer to the problems and needs you face, the things which appear impossible to you. But He is so real, so compassionate, so understanding, AND so practical that He both recognizes the mountain being there and the way to get it removed. That way is His covenant promise in the MIRACLE OF SEED-FAITH. In Matthew 17:20, Jesus says:

> If ye have faith as a grain of mustard seed, ye shall say unto this mountain, Remove hence to yonder place; and it shall remove; and nothing shall be impossible unto you.

As I stood fearful and trembling over the bills there in the crusade, ready to give up and walk out, I could have completely failed and I wouldn't be writing this book. Had Evelyn not made her faith as a seed planted, if she hadn't given of herself that evening, even though she was terribly embarrassed to do it, then no seed would have been planted . . . and there would have been no harvest — which is to say (since harvest and miracles mean the same thing in Bible terms) there would have been NO MIRACLE . . . no miracle, and Oral Roberts would have GIVEN UP.

Under the New Covenant a seed of faith is what you give God to work with IN THE SAME WAY A FARMER GIVES SEED TO THE EARTH TO WORK WITH TO BRING FORTH A HARVEST. And you've got to give a seed to match your need.

Well, Evelyn did, and I finally did, and God gave the harvest (THE MIRACLE).

What is in your life that you are threatened with? Is it like a fiery furnace or a mountain you can't climb?

Somebody in your household can do something that will be in harmony with the 3 Covenant Miracle Keys of Seed-Faith that our Lord has given us. These are 1) trust God as your Source, 2) sow seed for a miracle, and 3) expect a miracle. Maybe you can do something, or something within you can. Just as Evelyn had to swallow her pride and step forth and sow a seed of faith, you can do it.

When I think of how only six months after this ministry started, my fear could have ended it all, I still tremble a little. All those millions I've ministered to in crusades, on radio, on television, in my writings, the Oral Roberts University — none of this would have happened if Evelyn, my darling wife, had not in that pressure-packed moment let God use her in a miracle that saved this ministry.

Oh, the wonder of what a wife with faith in God can do for her husband! She would not give up!

Part IV

WHAT WILL YOU CHOOSE?
A MIRACLE OF HEALING FOR
BOB DEWEESE

MY CO-EVANGELIST DIED BUT WE STILL DID NOT GIVE UP

I remember when my co-evangelist, Bob DeWeese, who's been with me since 1951 in all the crusades and still holds partner meetings all over the country, had a heart attack a few months ago and died. He had a cardiac arrest and they finally brought him back with their medical equipment. Bob actually went into heaven. He saw the city and he heard them calling him to come back and he could hear them in the distance. But he was so filled with the glory in seeing the city of God he didn't want to come back. But by their scientific methods they brought him back and he lay there on the bed and finally they let some of us in, his family and me. And I went in and had a prayer with him. I did the best I could, or I thought I did. I knew the doctor who had really done a magnificent job on Bob. He is both a physician and a man filled with the Holy Spirit. After I had thanked him and the others, I went to get on the elevator with Collins Steele

At an ORU Covenant Family Seminar Bob DeWeese tells how he survived a heart attack because his granddaughter Cindy Did Not Give Up.

who joined the team the same year Bob did. Bob's granddaughter came up and took hold of my arm. She put my hands in hers and began to cry. And she said, "Brother Roberts, you didn't pray for my grandfather." I started to say, "Oh, but yes I did." But the Lord let me be silent. I didn't say anything and she said, "You didn't pray for my grandfather. That's my grandfather in there. I grew up in your meetings under the big tent and I saw you pray for the people and I saw people healed and you didn't pray a tent prayer."

As she held my hands in hers, she began to pump my arms up and down. I counted eight times that she raised my hands. I could tell she was dead serious, crying and saying, "You've got to go back in there and pray. You've got to go back in there and give him a tent prayer."

Now, you might not know what a tent prayer is, but Brother DeWeese told the story at one of our chapel services a couple of months ago, and I would like to share it with you just as he told it:

Well, I came home from preaching up in Des Moines at our conference, where I preached three times on Sunday. I came home Monday, and Tuesday morning I said, "I feel a little tired today." I didn't know why. Usually I don't have those feelings. I get sleep, then I'm ready to go. And I just felt tired.

Sometimes for exercise I play golf or tennis

or racquetball. When I play racquetball I try to play doubles because that's easier. Three friends and I were supposed to play racquetball on a court here in part of this building, but two of them didn't show up. So I am trying to keep up with this one young fellow who is very competitive. My word! I'm not going to let him know that a 30-year-old can beat a 68-year-old. So I'm in there battling it out and serving as hard as I could, when all of a sudden my feet flew out from under me and, bang, I hit the boards. I lay there a minute and I said, "How did that happen?" And I got up, brushed myself off, went on playing and pretty soon I began to feel something I'd never felt before. I felt a deep pain in my shoulder. Then I felt a little nauseous. Then I felt a cold sweat, and I went to look for Glen Smith our trainer, but he'd just left. I looked for Collins Steele but he'd just left. And I knew I was having a heart attack. Have you ever tried to call an ambulance for yourself? Try that sometime, will you? "Hey, I need an ambulance." "Who for?" "Me." You know.

So I struggled through a shower, got dressed, and went home. Charlotte my wife drove up just when I did and I said, "Honey, call the ambulance. I know that's what I need." She said, "What is it?" I said, "My heart." I walked in and lay down with this deep pain. I had never felt anything like it. There was deep pain in my arms and a lack of circulation.

So these wonderful medics (aren't they something?) in a little while came with the ambulance. By that time our campus doctor was there and a couple of the ORU Medical School doctors were there. Bob my son was there and Charlotte was committing me to God. I looked up at Charlotte and said, "Honey, I've got perfect peace, perfect peace. If this is it, praise the Lord. I don't have a fear." And you know, that's what it's all about, when you come up to something like that. Anybody can have faith in fair weather when everything's going great. But it's when you face a great need; you don't go hysterical and lose control, but keep your faith in God.

I just lay there and, oh, such peace filled me. Then the medics came and loaded me up into an ambulance. They took me up to intensive care and Dr. Basta, our beloved cardiologist, took over and did what he felt he should do, but my heart began to fibrillate and so he stayed right there for several hours trying to bring balance and stability. He told Mrs. DeWeese, "I don't know, I just don't know. There's something here I can't cope with right now."

I kind of went out of my head a little bit because of the medication and that worried my wife. Finally at eleven o'clock, I went to sleep in ICU and the doctor left. Have you ever been in ICU? They have a monitoring station out in the center of the unit and all of the opened rooms are round about so the nurses can monitor your heartbeat and get to you quickly. If you need help, they're right there.

About seven o'clock the next morning I came to and I saw the nurse standing by my bed. All of a sudden she raised her voice and then I passed out. What she was saying was, "Code blue, code blue, cardiac arrest." My heart stopped, my breathing stopped, I died.

Well, the next thing I knew, I was walking down a beautiful pathway. Oh, it was pretty. I was so loaded with life you can't believe it. I was saturated. I was permeated. I was scintillated. I felt great blessings of health and strength. I have never felt anything like that in my life. From my head to my toenails I was vibrating with life and power and peace — every care gone, every burden gone, every problem gone. Then I looked straight ahead and there was the New Jerusalem, the City of God. Oh, it was gorgeous, blue and white merging together, these beautiful buildings and all, and I was going for it as fast as I could go. Well, if they'd just left me alone a little longer, I'd have more to tell. But the next thing I knew the nurse was calling, "Mr. DeWeese."

There was a doctor eight feet from my bed

when I died, when my heart stopped and my breathing stopped, so he jumped on my chest and began pounding it. Nothing that they did could get me to respond. I was gone. So they brought in the electrodes that stop the fibrillation, that stop the quivering of the heart and let it try to get started all over again. They got it going, and when I started to come to I heard this awful noise. I couldn't figure out what the terrible noise was. It was the breathing machine. It was covering my face, breathing for me. Then I came to a little more. They finally took the breathing machine off. The room was full of doctors and nurses and I looked over at Dr. Basta and said, "Why did you bring me back to this mess? If you only knew where I've been, what I felt, what I saw! The battle was over! Victory was mine! Never another test or trial or problem of any kind. And now you brought me back to this and I've got to start all over again."

Well, pretty soon they let Charlotte come in and I saw her and motioned for her to come over. I was all broken up and homesick for heaven, and I said, "Honey, I've been over on the other side and I want to go back." She said, "Well, you can go back but not now."

A little while later Brother Roberts came in and prayed for me. I've prayed for hundreds of people in ICU and it's different than praying in

a room. You're right there with the doctors, the
nurses, the patients, and people all around you.
Prayer is urgently needed but with all due respect
it's not always a place where you pray with the
usual freedom you desire. When Brother Roberts
prayed I had lapsed partly back into unconscious-
ness but was aware of his prayer which was in a
very low voice. Charlotte was in the waiting room
with Bob and Donna, along with my granddaughter Cindy.

Oral walked by and said, "I don't know, I don't
know. I don't have the answer. I'll go on home.
I'm going to think and pray about this. I don't
have the answer." He went over to the elevator
with Collins Steele, when all of a sudden, Cindy,
my granddaughter, who was now 22, felt something happen to her. The Spirit of God came on
her.

Tears started bursting from her eyes and the
Holy Spirit took over in her life. She ran up to
Brother Roberts just as he was getting on the
elevator, grabbed his arms, and said, "Brother
Roberts, Brother Roberts, you didn't pray a miracle prayer for my grandfather. You didn't pray
the kind of a prayer you used to pray in the tent
crusades when the crippled were healed and the
blind saw and miracles happened. I want you to
go back and pray a tent miracle prayer for my
grandfather."

Oral was standing there, his eyes wide, looking at Cindy as she was pumping his arms up and down. Well, Brother Roberts got the answer.

He said, "All right, Cindy, let's go." And he had that look of an eagle on his face. He came back in that room and looked down at me. He got my attention and he said, "Bob, do you think God's through with you?"

I said, "Well, no, I guess not."

"All right," he said, "I'll pray for you if you don't think He's through with you. If you think He's through with you, I won't pray for you." But he said, "If you think God has something left for you to do, I'll pray for you."

And I said, "Yes, I do."

"All right," he said, "I want to ask you a question. You've always said you'd die about the same time your dad did." I'm two years older than he was when he died.

And I said, "Yeah, that's right."

Brother Roberts said, "I want to ask you this question, are you believing for your dad's genes or your mother's?"

She lived to be 94. I said, "I'll take Mom's."

"OK," and then he prayed one of those tent prayers for me. I tell you, when he was finished I was kicking and waving and the doctors were excited.

One doctor walked near there and said to one of the nurses, "You have got to stop this noise in here."

The nurse said, "You tell him, it's Oral Roberts."

I went back in two weeks and they gave me a monitoring test. They put a monitor on me and for 16 hours I did double the exercise I had been doing to see if there were any skipped beats, etc., but everything was OK.

So the doctor said, "All right, come back and see me in a month."

When I went back I said, "Hey, Dr. Basta, I'm feeling pretty good. Can I go back to work in September?"

He said, "Not September, not October, not November, maybe January."

I said, "Well, OK, you're the boss."

He gave me an EKG and then he said, "Now I want to give you a treadmill test."

I said, "OK." So he gave me a treadmill test and kept making it steeper and faster, and pretty soon he said to me, "Are you OK?" And I said, "I guess I am, I'm breathing out of my nose. When I work real hard I start breathing out of my mouth so I guess everything's OK."

He said, "I've never heard it explained like that before." So when he was finished he shook his head and said, "Go on back to work, and you can play tennis and golf, but no more racquetball."

I went back the other day and took another EKG. I'm in therapy down at the hospital. I was there this afternoon for an hour and a half. We do seven different things. We go treadmill to rowing machine to bicycle, monitors are on us all the time. I first started out walking a block and then a quarter of a mile, then a half mile and I finally got so I could walk completely around the campus, three miles in 39 minutes. That's pretty good walking, isn't it? So God has been gracious and wonderful, praise the Lord.

Bob is full-time in the ministry again as my co-evangelist. It would have been so easy to give up. I almost did for him. But Cindy kept pumping my arms and telling me to go back and pray like I know how to pray. She wouldn't give up.

Part V

THE MIRACLE OF
ORAL ROBERTS UNIVERSITY

THE MIRACLE OF ORAL ROBERTS
UNIVERSITY AND HOW IT WAS BUILT
FROM NOTHING BY NOT GIVING UP

"**O**RAL, YOU CAN'T DO IT!"

This emphatic warning came from a warm friend of many years and the pastor of one of our great churches in Tulsa. I knew that his words were really a sincere, earnest plea. What he was really saying was "Oral, don't try it, it's bigger than you are. I don't want to see you make a fool of yourself."

My friend was talking about the building of Oral Roberts University. We were starting to build — with NOTHING. We have never had any tangible assets to start a major building, and when we announced that we were going to build, people were fearful — including my friend. It just simply didn't look possible.

And from the standpoint of human reason my building a first-rate liberal arts university couldn't be done. But these people had no idea of what was inside me. I've never done anything of a major nature until God spoke to me. I'm not saying that He speaks to me every time in a loud voice but when He speaks to me it's clear enough that I understand Him. I don't take any steps — that is, initiated by myself — unless I hear from God. And I've always believed in doing things first-rate for God.

I'm very fortunate that right after my conversion and all through the years my mother kept saying to me:

"Oral, obey God."

She just drilled it into me: "Obey the Lord; obey the Lord; obey the Lord." Now this is how you begin to get needs met in your life — by obeying the Lord. I know. I've been down that road. The HOW will come. The important thing is to KNOW that the Lord is dealing with you and that the Lord wants you to do something.

When I was just a young man God had said — and I heard the words deep inside myself:

"BUILD ME A UNIVERSITY . . . BUILD IT ON MY POWER AND THE AUTHORITY OF THE HOLY SPIRIT."

And God said, "I will let you build it out of the same ingredient I used when I made the earth — NOTHING."

Can you imagine how I felt . . . having God say this to me right after my healing when I was just 17? I didn't understand . . . but I carried this dream in my heart, never doubting He wanted me to do it. I entered the healing ministry in 1947 and began this worldwide ministry of deliverance. All through those years of traveling in the continents of the world, of preaching to the masses, of being on national television and radio, it was in my mind . . .

"BUILD ME A UNIVERSITY . . ."

Of course I often wondered why God wanted ME to build a university. I had gone to college but did not have an earned doctorate. I was not into academics in any way, although I was studious in all respects.

But why would God want a man in the healing ministry to build a major university that would have a college of arts and sciences and graduate schools of business, theology, nursing, dentistry, medicine, law and education — why?

Then I began to understand as God revealed to me that He wanted me to bring healing to the whole man — spirit, mind, and body. And He wanted an education for the whole man — mind, spirit, and body. I knew that man is more than mind . . . he is more than spirit . . . he is more than physical — he is all three. He is like a circle. Anytime you touch a part of a circle you touch all of it. Whenever you touch a human being at any place in his existence, you touch all of him because you cannot separate his triune being. When God said to build a university and do it for the education of the whole man, I knew it would take the power of the Holy Spirit. But if I ever gave up, it would never be finished.

ORU's entrance — the Avenue of Flags

Aerial view of the campus of Oral Roberts University

In my heart God kept saying:

"BUILD ME A UNIVERSITY . . . THE HOW WILL COME . . . BUILD IT."

As far back as 1952 I drove by the property that is now the campus. My children were with me. I had them to get out of the car and we prayed, "God, hold this land for us to build Your university on."

The land was owned by an oil family. A number of people had tried to buy it, but this family didn't need to sell. But in 1962 — 10 years later — I felt impressed of the Lord to send our attorney to them to try to buy the land. And they said, "Yes, we'll sell it — we decided to yesterday." So we paid the smallest down payment possible on the land, dug some holes, and began to lay the foundations for the first buildings. We had very little money, really none if you considered how much it would cost to build a whole new university. We had no faculty, no students, and only a handful who believed that we could do it.

OUR PERSONAL COMMITMENT TO ORU

I had continued on the "love-offering plan" as a means of personal support until about 1960. At that time, my wife Evelyn and I felt directed to go on a set salary. We decided to give one-half of what we had saved over the years to ORU, and the other half to our four children for their education. After much prayer I discussed this with my team, then with the board of trustees of our evangelistic association.

With everyone understanding the decision, I went on a set salary. I have been just as happy as I was before. I have learned that in order to progress, a Christian has to change, not in principle but in method. It is not always easy to do but it is absolutely necessary for growth in Christ.

A DAY OF TRIUMPH

On September 7, 1965, we welcomed our first freshman class of 300 to ORU. In my opening address I challenged the students:

> In the history of the human family, there has been only one complete whole man. This was Jesus of Nazareth. Our concept of the whole man is derived from His life and from the example He left us. Combining what we know about Him with the most modern techniques of higher education, we have brought into being this new University and through it, we reach for wholeness.

> While others are reaching for a ride to the moon, you will reach for a whole life.

> ORU is a daring new concept in higher education. It was planned from the beginning to innovate change in all three basic aspects of your being — the intellectual, the physical, and the spiritual.

> There's an education here for your mind, for without the development of your intellect you cannot be a complete person.

There's an education here for your body, for that too is essential to your development as a whole person. Jesus is our great example. He is personified health and vitality.

There is a unique opportunity here for an education or development of your inner man, for the most important part of you is your spirit.

The world doesn't need more college students to wave flags, carry placards, halt traffic, and riot against law and order. What our civilization needs is that you will make your spiritual development a normal part of your education and your life.

You can emerge as the world's most wanted college graduates. A healthy body that you know how to take care of, a trained and disciplined mind that never settles for less than excellence, governed by an invincible spirit of integrity, inspired by a personal relationship with a living God, and driven by an irresistible desire to be a whole man to make a troubled world whole again!

The second year, 546 students were enrolled. It was happening because I DID NOT GIVE UP!

APRIL 2, 1967 — A DAY TO REMEMBER . . .

One of the great days in our lives was the dedication of Oral Roberts University. More than 18,000 people came from all over the United States, Canada, and from several foreign countries to attend the service that lasted a little over two hours! The main speaker was my warm friend, Dr. Billy Graham.

The ceremony was to begin at 2:30 p.m. and by noon traffic was backed up for miles in either direction of the 500-acre campus. Not to be outdone by the traffic snarl, hundreds of Tulsans stayed at home to watch the impressive outdoor ceremonies on local television.

Local as well as national VIPs were on hand to observe firsthand our dream of a lifetime — a high-caliber university of academic excellence, where Christ is the center of all learning.

Faithful partners of the Oral Roberts Ministry were present to share the greatness of the moment, with the students they had helped to sponsor, in a setting they had helped to build. They were a part of history and they knew it. This was a day of fulfillment for the ministry they loved. Pride seemed to be bursting at the seams as many expressed their heartfelt sentiments. Several mentioned, "This is the most exciting moment of my life!"

In his dedicatory address Billy Graham said, "This certainly is the university of tomorrow. Evangelical Christendom can be proud today of this university and what it will mean to the future of this country . . . May ORU produce a holy enthusiasm for the will of God. It's still true that people who get excited about the Scriptures and the will of God are people who can change the world . . . To this end we dedicate ORU."

Dr. Billy Graham, our beloved friend, was the main speaker at the ORU dedication ceremonies. He told the crowd of more than 18,000 people — "This certainly is the university of tomorrow. Evangelical Christendom can be proud of this university."

Later Billy said to me, "Oral, be tough with ORU."

I said, "What do you mean, Billy?"

He said, "Be tough with the students and faculty; be tough with your standards and principles; be tough." He added, "That's the only way God will bless the school."

I believe it. I'm dedicated to obeying God so He can use everything about the school to change young lives and set them on fire for the Lord and teach them NOT TO GIVE UP IN THEIR LIVES. A WINNER NEVER QUITS AND A QUITTER NEVER WINS.

THE MIRACLE OF ACCREDITATION

Even before we opened the doors of ORU in 1965 we had already begun the process of receiving accreditation with the North Central Association of Colleges and Secondary Schools. Again the skeptics said, "You can't do it."

I've heard that all my life. "You can't do it." It's like waving a red flag in front of me because God had said, "Build Me a university . . ."

On the other hand, God has His own ways of encouraging me and letting me know that He truly has spoken to me.

A man from Canada, whom I've never met, wrote me a letter. In it was a check. He said:

Oral Roberts,

I'm sending you this money to help build the

university on the Holy Spirit. God spoke to me and told me to help a man by the name of Oral Roberts to build Him a university. So here is the money. I don't know why I'm sending it because I really don't like you. But God spoke to me. It's all the money I have.

I called my men together and read the letter to them. There was quite a substantial check in it and we said, "Let's send it back to him if it's all the money the man has. He might go hungry." Then we read the letter again and we saw a deeper meaning. The man was saying to me, "Don't think I sent the money to you. I sent it because God told me to send it, because He wants a university built on the Holy Spirit. He will take care of me."

As I said, we had begun to apply for accreditation. And they began to lay the rules and regulations down to us . . . you can't do this and you can't do that. We finally reached the point where we stood face-to-face with the people from the North Central Association that accredits the universities in this district. Face-to-face and toe-to-toe we said, "This is the way we are to build it: academically, strong and sound; physically, for the development of our bodies; and spiritually, God first."

"Are you going to teach evolution?" they asked. "Well, yes, we will teach everything that we can find that man has taught about evolution and tell it to our students."

"You will?"

"Yes. But we will also say, 'Now THIS is what we believe.'"

These were great educators — PhDs — very respectful but very tough, and one of them said, "Well, my idea of a college is that a kid comes here and we throw everything at him we can to try to destroy his faith in God." He said, "Mr. President, what do you have to say to that?"

Before I could answer, our academic dean said, "Let me answer that. We at Oral Roberts University do not believe that we have a right to destroy anybody's faith in God. Rather, we will try to establish his faith in God."

The chairman of that committee turned to this PhD and said, "You've said enough. Let's talk about something else." So we moved off that subject.

They wound up saying, "This is what we will do. You have met our standards of academics. (We had *more* than met every standard.) Every building is more than is needed. The library is greater. The PhDs are more, the program is more. (They admitted that.) But all these other things, that's your business."

And they finally admitted, "It IS your business. Our business is your academic affairs. Your business is what you preach — your philosophy. We will require you, however, to live up to your philosophy."

Inside I was saying, "Thank You, God, thank You.

They are going to require us to live up to our spiritual standards." This is the North Central Association of Colleges and Secondary Schools. I mean, you couldn't beat that if you tried. We can't change, because the North Central Association is demanding we live up to our spiritual standards.

So on Wednesday, March 31, 1971 — just six short years after the university had opened its doors — we were notified that Oral Roberts University had been granted full accreditation by the North Central Association of Colleges and Secondary Schools. This university is one of the few colleges ever to have achieved full accreditation in this length of time — and one of the very few private institutions ever to be granted the full ten-year term when first accredited, and that, by unanimous decision. It was a day of victory! ! ! Another miracle! *We didn't give up* when the going got rough. We kept our eyes on Jesus as our Source.

The John D. Messick Learning Resources Center, named in honor of the renowned dean of academic affairs.

ORU'S faculty, staff, and students gather on the ORU campus. The ORU student body has grown from its first class of 300 students in 1965 to its present enrollment of over 4,000 students.

The heartbeat of ORU — the Prayer Tower

Entrance to ORU's University Village, a retirement center for senior citizens, adjacent to the campus.

March 31, 1971 — a day I'll never forget! With the announcement of ORU's full accreditation, students picked me up and carried me out of chapel in a triumphant processional. The full accreditation by the North Central Association of Colleges and Secondary Schools was granted less than six years after ORU opened its doors, one of the fastest accreditations on record!

Part VI

DON'T *YOU* GIVE UP

Not long ago, when the City of Faith structure was about half completed, someone asked me how the money was coming in. "Well, we are running a little short right now," I replied.

"Is what you have completed paid for?" the man asked.

"Yes," I answered. "We are paying for it as we build. This is what God told me to do so we can open it debt-free."

"Well, stop right there. Don't even worry about the rest of the building project. You have already done more than anybody else has ever done by getting it this far."

What he said was true. God has helped us get the City of Faith to the point where it is now. But it is not finished and I refuse to quit until it is. I will not give up. When God told me to build the City of Faith, He was explicit in His instructions. Nowhere, at any time, did He include plans for us to retreat. He said, "Do it! DO IT ALL AS I TOLD YOU TO DO!"

I'll obey His voice. We will not compromise. By His help, it will be finished . . . ON SCHEDULE!

Partner, I know you have REAL PROBLEMS. But are they any more real than the furnace of fire faced by the young Hebrews? That fire was as real as the paper this book is written on. And . . . it had been heated seven times hotter than ever before just for these three boys.

The king reminded them of that fact as he jeeringly asked them who was the God who could deliver them from his furnace. "Do you really think He will deliver you?" the king asked.

The answer came back. "We know our God is able to deliver us from both the burning, fiery furnace and from your hand, O King. But whether He does or not, we want you to know, WE WILL NOT BOW DOWN to your image!"

As they were thrown into the furnace they loosed their faith to God and, instead of being destroyed by the flames, they were rewarded by meeting the Son of God. They met Him face-to-face as the Fourth Man in the midst of the burning, fiery furnace. *WHEN FEAR KNOCKS* AT YOUR DOOR, *ALWAYS LET FAITH ANSWER* THAT DOOR!

What I am saying is very simple. Give in to doubt and fear, and your life will be dominated from now

Scale Model

The City of Faith, Tulsa, Oklahoma
Scheduled opening is November 1, 1981.

on. The devil will try to drive you out of your mind.
FACE YOUR PROBLEMS HEAD-ON, TRUST GOD
AS YOUR SOURCE, AND YOUR FAITH WILL
TAKE ON A NEW DIMENSION! I literally live by
this power of faith . . . and I believe YOU CAN TOO.

You may be going through a severe trial right
now . . . or it may come to you tomorrow. But I am
impressed to tell you, "DO NOT GIVE UP! DO
NOT BOW DOWN!"

I feel your deliverance is on the way. Your covenant rights in God are just too vital to give up without a fight. God wants to meet you at this moment
at the point of the need you have! I believe I can
help you if you will let me.

Just write me:

Oral Roberts
Tulsa, Oklahoma 74171

I'll be honored to receive your letter, pray for your
needs, and write you back. Use the prayer sheet on
the next page. This is a ministry of faith and prayer
and I'd love to hear from you. Let's both look to God.

DON'T GIVE UP!

Brother Roberts, please pray for:

_____

_____

_____

_____

_____

_____

☐ I'm already in the Covenant Family.

☐ I want to join your Covenant Family. Please send me full details.

☐ I'm enclosing $_____ to help you in the work God has called you to do.

I'M NOT GIVING UP

NAME_____

779

ADDRESS_____

CITY_____STATE_____ZIP_____

Mail to: Oral Roberts, Tulsa, Oklahoma 74171

This is my brother Vaden and me (I'm on the right). If God could raise me up from poverty, from stammering and stuttering, and then heal me of tuberculosis — He can perform miracles for anybody. No matter what you're feeling, Don't Give Up.

WE WANT

TO BE AS CLOSE TO YOU

AS YOU'LL LET US BE.

Always remember

what Oral Roberts told you

in this book:

DON'T GIVE UP!

Oral Roberts

Evelyn Roberts